## DOVER · THRIFT · EDITIONS

# Early Poems

# WILLIAM CARLOS WILLIAMS

## DOVER PUBLICATIONS, INC.
### Mineola, New York

# DOVER THRIFT EDITIONS

GENERAL EDITOR: STANLEY APPELBAUM
EDITOR OF THIS VOLUME: RICHARD KOSS

## *Bibliographical Note*

This Dover edition, first published in 1997, contains a new selection of poems from the following William Carlos Williams volumes: *Al Que Quiere!* The Four Seas Co., Boston, 1917; *Sour Grapes,* The Four Seas Co., Boston, 1921; *The Tempers,* Elkin Mathews, London, 1913; as well as from the following periodicals: *The Dial,* August, 1920; *Poetry Magazine,* November, 1916 and *The Little Review,* January, 1920. A new introductory Note has been prepared specially for this edition.

## *Library of Congress Cataloging-in-Publication Data*

Williams, William Carlos, 1883–1963.
    Early poems / William Carlos Williams.
        p.    cm. — (Dover thrift editions)
    ISBN 0-486-29294-0 (pbk.)
    I. Title.   II. Series.
PS3545.I544A6   1997
811'.52—dc21
                                                            97-10947
                                                            CIP

Manufactured in the United States of America
Dover Publications, Inc., 31 East 2nd Street, Mineola, N.Y. 11501

# Note

WILLIAM CARLOS WILLIAMS was born in 1883 in Rutherford, New Jersey, the small, industrial town in which he lived, wrote, practiced medicine and died in 1963. Educated first at the Chateau de Lancy in Geneva, then at the Horace Mann School in Manhattan, Williams attended medical school at the University of Pennsylvania from 1902 to 1906. It was there that he first met Ezra Pound, then an undergraduate, and the two formed a lifelong, if occasionally strained, friendship.

Pound encouraged Williams's early writing, recommending the latter's poems to *Poetry* magazine of Chicago and arranging in 1913 for the London publication of *The Tempers*, for which Pound furnished an introduction—as well as a glowing review of the volume! If Williams, who by then had married and settled into the successful pediatric practice that would keep him close to his Rutherford roots, was not a *de facto* member of Pound's budding imagist circle in London (which included Hilda Doolittle and Richard Aldington), he was something of a fellow traveler. Indeed, imagism's exaltation of a poetry that approached its subject directly, unencumbered by superfluous words or rigid, metronomic rhythms was to find its distant echo in Williams's celebrated call for "no ideas but in things" in his epic poem *Paterson*.

Williams's insistence on working in the idiom of modern American speech and on mining local terrain for his poems, however, veered sharply from the classical allusions and Far Eastern experimentations of Pound and his imagist set. These nativist affinities recall the poetry of Walt Whitman, and while Williams was never entirely comfortable with such comparisons, many of the poems in *Al Que Quiere!* (or "To Him Who Wants It") and *Sour Grapes* suggest Whitman's particular warmth and generosity of spirit for the ordinary, the commonplace and the American.

Influenced by imagist theories of Pound and the nativist sensibilities of Whitman, William Carlos Williams found his singular voice. This selection of his early poetry captures the artist as he came into his own and provides a glimpse of one of the greatest American poets of the twentieth century.

# Contents

# FROM "AL QUE QUIERE!"

## DANSE RUSSE

If I when my wife is sleeping
and the baby and Kathleen
are sleeping
and the sun is a flame-white disc
in silken mists
above shining trees,—
if I in my north room
danse naked, grotesquely
before my mirror
waving my shirt round my head
and singing softly to myself:
"I am lonely, lonely.
I was born to be lonely.
I am best so!"
If I admire my arms, my face
my shoulders, flanks, buttocks
against the yellow drawn shades,—

who shall say I am not
the happy genius of my household?

## TRACT

I will teach you my townspeople
how to perform a funeral—
for you have it over a troop
of artists—
unless one should scour the world—
you have the ground sense necessary.

See! the hearse leads.
I begin with a design for a hearse.
For Christ's sake not black—
nor white either—and not polished!
Let it be weathered—like a farm wagon—
with gilt wheels (this could be
applied fresh at small expense)
or no wheels at all:
a rough day to drag over the ground.

Knock the glass out!
My God—glass, my townspeople!
For what purpose? Is it for the dead
to look out or for us to see
how well he is housed or to see
the flowers or the lack of them—
or what?
To keep the rain and snow from him?
He will have a heavier rain soon:
pebbles and dirt and what not.
Let there be no glass—
and no upholstery phew!
and no little brass rollers
and small easy wheels on the bottom—
my townspeople what are you thinking of?

A rough plain hearse then
with gilt wheels and no top at all
On this the coffin lies
by its own weight.

                        No wreathes please—
especially no hot house flowers.
Some common memento is better,
something he prized and is known by:
his old clothes—a few books perhaps—
God knows what! You realize
how we are about these things
my townspeople—
something will be found—anything
even flowers if he had come to that.

So much for the hearse.
For heaven's sake though see to the driver!
Take off the silk hat! In fact
that's no place at all for him—
up there unceremoniously
dragging our friend out to his own dignity!
Bring him down—bring him down!
Low and inconspicuous! I'd not have him ride
on the wagon at all—damn him—
the undertaker's understrapper!
Let him hold the reins
and walk at the side
and inconspicuously too!

Then briefly as to yourselves:
Walk behind—as they do in France,
seventh class, or if you ride
Hell take curtains! Go with some show
of inconvenience; sit openly—
to the weather as to grief.
Or do you think you can shut grief in?
What—from us? We who have perhaps
nothing to lose? Share with us
share with us—it will be money
in your pockets.
                              Go now
I think you are ready.


## SUB TERRA

Where shall I find you,
you my grotesque fellows
that I seek everywhere
to make up my band?
None, not one
with the earthy tastes I require;
the burrowing pride that rises
subtly as on a bush in May.

Where are you this day,
you my seven year locusts
with cased wings?
Ah my beauties how I long—!
That harvest
that shall be your advent—
thrusting up through the grass,
up under the weeds
answering me,
*that* shall be satisfying!
The light shall leap and snap
that day as with a million lashes!

Oh, I have you; yes
you are about me in a sense:
playing under the blue pools
that are my windows,—
but they shut you out still,
there in the half light.
For the simple truth is
that though I see you clear enough
you are not there!

It is not that—it is you,
you I want!

—God, if I could fathom the guts of shadows!

You to come with me
poking into negro houses
with their gloom and smell!
In among children
leaping around a dead dog!
Mimicking
onto the lawns of the rich!
You!
to go with me a-tip-toe,
head down under heaven,
nostrils lipping the wind!

## PASTORAL

When I was younger
it was plain to me
I must make something of myself.
Older now
I walk back streets
admiring the houses
of the very poor:
roof out of line with sides
the yards cluttered
with old chicken wire, ashes,
furniture gone wrong;
the fences and outhouses
built of barrel-staves
and parts of boxes, all,
if I am fortunate,
smeared a bluish green
that properly weathered
pleases me best
of all colors.

               No one
will believe this
of vast import to the nation.

## METRIC FIGURE

There is a bird in the poplars!
It is the sun!
The leaves are little yellow fish
swimming in the river.
The bird skims above them,
day is on his wings.
Phœbus!
It is he that is making
the great gleam among the poplars!
It is his singing
outshines the noise
of leaves clashing in the wind.

## WOMAN WALKING

An oblique cloud of purple smoke
across a milky silhouette
of house sides and tiny trees—
a little village—
that ends in a saw edge
of mist-covered trees
on a sheet of grey sky.

To the right, jutting in,
a dark crimson corner of roof.
To the left, half a tree:

　　—what a blessing it is
to see you in the street again,
powerful woman,
coming with swinging haunches,
breasts straight forward,
supple shoulders, full arms
and strong, soft hands (I've felt them)
carrying the heavy basket.
I might well see you oftener!
And for a different reason
than the fresh eggs
you bring us so regularly.

Yes, you, young as I,
with boney brows,
kind grey eyes and a kind mouth;
you walking out toward me
from that dead hillside!
I might well see you oftener.

## GULLS

My townspeople, beyond in the great world,
are many with whom it were far more
profitable for me to live than here with you.
These whirr about me calling, calling!

and for my own part I answer them, loud as I can,
but they, being free, pass!
I remain! Therefore, listen!
For you will not soon have another singer.

First I say this: you have seen
the strange birds, have you not, that sometimes
rest upon our river in winter?
Let them cause you to think well then of the storms
that drive many to shelter. These things
do not happen without reason.

And the next thing I say is this:
I saw an eagle once circling against the clouds
over one of our principal churches—
Easter, it was—a beautiful day!—:
three gulls came from above the river
and crossed slowly seaward!
Oh, I know you have your own hymns, I have heard them—
and because I knew they invoked some great protector
I could not be angry with you, no matter
how much they outraged true music—

You see, it is not necessary for us to leap at each other,
and, as I told you, in the end
the gulls moved seaward very quietly.

## IN HARBOR

Surely there, among the great docks, is peace, my mind;
there with the ships moored in the river.
Go out, timid child,
and snuggle in among the great ships talking so quietly.
Maybe you will even fall asleep near them and be
lifted into one of their laps, and in the morning—
There is always the morning in which to remember it all!
Of what are they gossiping? God knows.
And God knows it matters little for we cannot understand them.
Yet it is certainly of the sea, of that there can be no question.
It is a quiet sound. Rest! That's all I care for now.

The smell of them will put us to sleep presently.
Smell! It is the sea water mingling here into the river—
at least so it seems—perhaps it is something else—but what matter?

The sea water! It is quiet and smooth here!
How slowly they move, little by little trying
the hawsers that drop and groan with their agony.
Yes, it is certainly of the high sea they are talking.

## WINTER SUNSET

Then I raised my head
and stared out over
the blue February waste
to the blue bank of hill
with stars on it
in strings and festoons—
but above that:
one opaque
stone of a cloud
just on the hill
left and right
as far as I could see;
and above that
a red streak, then
icy blue sky!

It was a fearful thing
to come into a man's heart
at that time: that stone
over the little blinking stars
they'd set there.

## LOVE SONG

Daisies are broken
petals are news of the day
stems lift to the grass tops
they catch on shoes

part in the middle
leave root and leaves secure.

Black branches
carry square leaves
to the wood's top.
They hold firm
break with a roar
show the white!

Your moods are slow
the shedding of leaves
and sure
the return in May!

We walked
in your father's grove
and saw the great oaks
lying with roots
ripped from the ground.

## EL HOMBRE

It's a strange courage
you give me ancient star:

Shine alone in the sunrise
toward which you lend no part!

## LIBERTAD! IGUALDAD! FRATERNIDAD!

You sullen pig of a man
you force me into the mud
with your stinking ash-cart!

Brother!
      —if we were rich
we'd stick our chests out
and hold our heads high!

It is dreams that have destroyed us.

There is no more pride
in horses or in rein holding.
We sit hunched together brooding
our fate.

      Well—
all things turn bitter in the end
whether you choose the right or
the left way
         and—
dreams are not a bad thing.

## CANTHARA

The old black-man showed me
how he had been shocked
in his youth
by six women, dancing
a set-dance, stark naked below
the skirts raised round
their breasts:
      bellies flung foward
knees flying!
         —while
his gestures, against the
tiled wall of the dingy bath-room,
swished with ecstasy to
the familiar music of
         his old emotion.

## LOVE SONG

Sweep the house clean,
hang fresh curtains
in the windows
put on a new dress
and come with me!
The elm is scattering

its little loaves
of sweet smells
from a white sky!

Who shall hear of us
in the time to come?
Let him say there was
a burst of fragrance
from black branches.

## A PRELUDE

I know only the bare rocks of today.
In these lies my brown sea-weed,—
green quartz veins bent through the wet shale;
in these lie my pools left by the tide—
quiet, forgetting waves;
on these stiffen white star fish;
on these I slip bare footed!

Whispers of the fishy air touch my body;
"Sisters," I say to them.

## WINTER QUIET

Limb to limb, mouth to mouth
with the bleached grass
silver mist lies upon the back yards
among the outhouses.
                          The dwarf trees
pirouette awkwardly to it—
whirling round on one toe;
the big tree smiles and glances
                                   upward!
Tense with suppressed excitement
the fences watch where the ground
has humped an aching shoulder for
                              the ecstasy.

## DAWN

Ecstatic bird songs pound
the hollow vastness of the sky
with metallic clinkings—
beating color up into it
at a far edge,—beating it, beating it
with rising, triumphant ardor,—
stirring it into warmth,
quickening in it a spreading change,—
bursting wildly against it as
dividing the horizon, a heavy sun
lifts himself—is lifted—
bit by bit above the edge
of things,—runs free at last
out into the open—! lumbering
glorified in full release upward—
                                    songs cease.

## GOOD NIGHT

In brilliant gas light
I turn the kitchen spigot
and watch the water plash
into the clean white sink.
On the grooved drain-board
to one side is
a glass filled with parsley—
crisped green.
                    Waiting
for the water to freshen—
I glance at the spotless floor—:
a pair of rubber sandals
lie side by side
under the wall-table,
all is in order for the night.

Waiting, with a glass in my hand
—three girls in crimson satin
pass close before me on

the murmurous background of
the crowded opera—
                              it is
memory playing the clown—
three vague, meaningless girls
full of smells and
the rustling sound of
cloth rubbing on cloth and
little slippers on carpet—
high-school French
spoken in a loud voice!

Parsley in a glass,
still and shining,
brings me back. I take my drink
and yawn deliciously.
I am ready for bed.

## PORTRAIT OF A WOMAN IN BED

There's my things
drying in the corner:
that blue skirt
joined to the grey shirt—

I'm sick of trouble!
Lift the covers
if you want me
and you'll see
the rest of my clothes—
though it would be cold
lying with nothing on!

I won't work
and I've got no cash.
What are you going to do
about it?
—and no jewelry
(the crazy fools)

But I've my two eyes
and a smooth face
and here's this! look!
it's high!
There's brains and blood
in there—
my name's Robitza!
Corsets
can go to the devil—
and drawers along with them!
What do I care!

My two boys?
—they're keen!
Let the rich lady
care for them—
they'll beat the school
or
let them go to the gutter—
that ends trouble.

This house is empty
isn't it?
Then it's mine
because I need it.
Oh, I won't starve
while there's the Bible
to make them feed me.

Try to help me
if you want trouble
or leave me alone—
that ends trouble.

The county physician
is a damned fool
and you
can go to hell!

You could have closed the door
when you came in;
do it when you go out.
I'm tired.


## VIRTUE

Now? Why—
whirl-pools of
orange and purple flame
feather twists of chrome
on a green ground
funneling down upon
the steaming phallus-head
of the mad sun himself—
blackened crimson!
                              Now?

Why—
it is the smile of her
the smell of her
the vulgar inviting mouth of her!
It is—Oh, nothing new
nothing that lasts
an eternity, nothing worth
putting out to interest,
nothing—
but the fixing of an eye
concretely upon emptiness!

Come! here are—
cross-eyed men, a boy
with a patch, men walking
in their shirts, men in hats
dark men, a pale man
with little black moustaches
and a dirty white coat,
fat men with pudgy faces,
thin faces, crooked faces
slit eyes, grey eyes, black eyes

old men with dirty beards,
men in vests with
gold watch chains. Come!


## KELLER GEGEN DOM

Witness, would you—
one more young man
in the evening of his love
hurrying to confession:
steps down a gutter
crosses a street
goes in at a doorway
opens for you—
like some great flower—
a room filled with lamplight;
or whirls himself
obediently to
the curl of a hill
some wind-dancing afternoon;
lies for you in
the futile darkness of
a wall, sets stars dancing
to the crack of a leaf—

and—leaning his head away—
snuffs (secretly)
the bitter powder from
his thumb's hollow,
takes your blessing and
goes home to bed?

Witness instead
whether you like it or not
a dark vinegar smelling place
from which trickles
the chuckle of
beginning laughter

It strikes midnight.

## SMELL!

Oh strong ridged and deeply hollowed
nose of mine! what will you not be smelling?
What tactless asses we are, you and I, boney nose,
always indiscriminate, always unashamed,
and now it is the souring flowers of the bedraggled
poplars: a festering pulp on the wet earth
beneath them. With what deep thirst
we quicken our desires
to that rank odor of a passing springtime!
Can you not be decent? Can you not reserve your ardors
for something less unlovely? What girl will care
for us, do you think, if we continue in these ways?
Must you taste everything? Must you know everything?
Must you have a part in everything?

## BALLET

Are you not weary,
great gold cross
shining in the wind—
are you not weary
of seeing the stars
turning over you
and the sun
going to his rest
and you frozen with
a great lie
that leaves you
rigid as a knight
on a marble coffin?

—and you,
higher, still,
               robin,
untwisting a song
from the bare
top-twigs,
are you not

weary of labor,
even the labor of
a song?

Come down—join me
for I am lonely.

First it will be
a quiet pace
to ease our stiffness
but as the west yellows
you will be ready!

Here in the middle
of the roadway
we will fling
ourselves round
with dust lilies
till we are bound in
their twining stems!
We will tear
their flowers
with arms flashing!

And when
the astonished stars
push aside
their curtains
they will see us
fall exhausted where
wheels and
the pounding feet
of horses
will crush forth
our laughter.

## THE OGRE

Sweet child,
little girl with well shaped legs

you cannot touch the thoughts
I put over and under and around you.
This is fortunate for they would
burn you to an ash otherwise.
Your petals would be quite curled up.

This is all beyond you—no doubt,
yet you do feel the brushings
of the fine needles;
the tentative lines of your whole body
prove it to me;
so does your fear of me,
your shyness;
likewise the toy baby cart
that you are pushing—
and besides, mother has begun
to dress your hair in a knot.
These are my excuses.

## THE OLD MEN

Old men who have studied
every leg show
in the city
Old men cut from touch
by the perfumed music—
polished or fleeced skulls
that stand before
the whole theater
in silent attitudes
of attention,—
old men who have taken precedence
over young men
and even over dark-faced
husbands whose minds
are a street with arc-lights.
Solitary old men for whom
we find no excuses—
I bow my head in shame
for those who malign you.

Old men
the peaceful beer of impotence
be yours!


## PASTORAL

If I say I have heard voices
who will believe me?

"None has dipped his hand
in the black waters of the sky
nor picked the yellow lilies
that sway on their clear stems
and no tree has waited
long enough nor still enough
to touch fingers with the moon."

I looked and there were little frogs
with puffed out throats,
singing in the slime.


## SPRING STRAINS

In a tissue-thin monotone of blue-grey buds
crowded erect with desire against
the sky—
                tense blue-grey twigs
slenderly anchoring them down, drawing
them in—
                two blue-grey birds chasing
a third struggle in circles, angles,
swift convergings to a point that bursts
instantly!
                Vibrant bowing limbs
pull downward, sucking in the sky
that bulges from behind, plastering itself
against them in packed rifts, rock blue
and dirty orange!
                But—
(Hold hard, rigid jointed trees!)

the blinding and red-edged sun-blur—
creeping energy, concentrated
counterforce—welds sky, buds, trees,
rivets them in one puckering hold!
Sticks through! Pulls the whole
counter-pulling mass upward, to the right,
locks even the opaque, not yet defined
ground in a terrific drag that is
loosening the very tap-roots!

On a tissue-thin monotone of blue-grey buds
two blue-grey girds, chasing a third,
at full cry! Now they are
flung outward and up—disappearing suddenly!

## A PORTRAIT IN GREYS

Will it never be possible
to separate you from your greyness?
Must you be always sinking backward
into your grey-brown landscapes—and trees
always in the distance, always against
a grey sky?
                    Must I be always
moving counter to you? Is there no place
where we can be at peace together
and the motion of our drawing apart
be altogether taken up?
                              I see myself
standing upon your shoulders touching
a grey, broken sky—
but you, weighted down with me,
yet gripping my ankles,—move
                              laboriously on,
where it is level and undisturbed by colors.

## TO A SOLITARY DISCIPLE

Rather notice, mon cher,
that the moon is

tilted above
the point of the steeple
than that its color
is shell-pink.

Rather observe
that it is early morning
than that the sky
is smooth
as a turquoise.

Rather grasp
how the dark
converging lines
of the steeple
meet at the pinnacle—
perceive how
its little ornament
tries to stop them—

See how it fails!
See how the converging lines
of the hexagonal spire
escape upward—
receding, dividing!
—sepals
that guard and contain
the flower!

Observe
how motionless
the eaten moon
lies in the protecting lines.

It is true:
in the light colors
of morning
brown-stone and slate
shine orange and dark blue.

But observe
the oppressive weight
of the squat edifice!
Observe
the jasmine lightness
of the moon.


## DEDICATION FOR A PLOT OF GROUND

This plot of ground
facing the waters of this inlet
is dedicated to the living presence of
Emily Richardson Wellcome
who was born in England; married;
lost her husband and with
her five year old son
sailed for New York in a two-master;
was driven to the Azores;
ran adrift on Fire Island shoal,
met her second husband
in a Brooklyn boarding house,
went with him to Puerto Rico
bore three more children, lost
her second husband, lived hard
for eight years in St. Thomas,
Puerto Rico, San Domingo, followed
the oldest son to New York,
lost her daughter, lost her "baby,"
seized the two boys of
the oldest son by the second marriage
mothered them—they being
motherless—fought for them
against the other grandmother
and the aunts, brought them here
summer after summer, defended
herself here against thieves,
storms, sun, fire,
against flies, against girls
that came smelling about, against
drought, against weeds, storm-tides,

neighbors, weasles that stole her chickens,
against the weakness of her own hands,
against the growing strength of
the boys, against wind, against
the stones, against trespassers,
against rents, against her own mind.

She grubbed this earth with her own hands,
domineered over this grass plot,
blackguarded her oldest son
into buying it, lived here fifteen years,
attained a final loneliness and—

If you can bring nothing to this place
but your carcass, keep out.

## LOVE SONG

I lie here thinking of you:—

the stain of love
is upon the world!
Yellow, yellow, yellow
it eats into the leaves,
smears with saffron
the horned branches that lean
heavily
against a smooth purple sky!
There is no light
only a honey-thick stain
that drips from leaf to leaf
and limb to limb
spoiling the colors
of the whole world—

you far off there under
the wine-red selvage of the west!

# FROM "THE TEMPERS"

## PEACE ON EARTH

The Archer is wake!
The Swan is flying!
Gold against blue
An Arrow is lying.
There is hunting in heaven—
Sleep safe till to-morrow.

The Bears are abroad!
The Eagle is screaming!
Gold against blue
Their eyes are gleaming!
Sleep!
Sleep safe till to-morrow.

The Sisters lie
With their arms intertwining;
Gold against blue
Their hair is shining!
The Serpent writhes!
Orion is listening!
Gold against blue
His sword is glistening!
Sleep!
There is hunting in heaven—
Sleep safe till to-morrow.

## POSTLUDE

Now that I have cooled to you
Let there be gold of tarnished masonry,
Temples soothed by the sun to ruin
That sleep utterly.
Give me hand for the dances,
Ripples at Philae, in and out,
And lips, my Lesbian,
Wall flowers that once were flame.

Your hair is my Carthage
And my arms the bow,
And our words arrows
To shoot the stars
Who from that misty sea
Swarm to destroy us.

But you there beside me—
Oh how shall I defy you,
Who wound me in the night
With breasts shining
Like Venus and like Mars?
The night that is shouting Jason
When the loud eaves rattle
As with waves above me
Blue at the prow of my desire.

## FIRST PRAISE

Lady of duskwood fastnesses,
    Thou art my Lady.
I have known the crisp splintering leaf-tread with thee on before,
White, slender through green saplings;
I have lain by thee on the grey forest floor
    Beside thee, my Lady.

Lady of rivers strewn with stones,
    Only thou art my Lady.
Where thousand the freshets are crowded like peasants to a fair;

Clearskinned, wild from seclusion,
They jostle whitearmed down the tent-bordered thoroughfare
    Praising my Lady.

## HOMAGE

Elvira, by love's grace
There goeth before you
A clear radiance
Which maketh all vain souls
Candles when noon is.

The loud clangour of pretenders
Melteth before you
Like the roll of carts passing,
But you come silently
And homage is given.

Now the little by-path
Which leadeth to love
Is again joyful with its many;
And the great highway
From love
Is without passers.

## FROM "THE BIRTH OF VENUS," SONG

Come with us and play!
See, we have breasts as women!
    From your tents by the sea
Come play with us: it is forbidden!

Come with us and play!
Lo, bare, straight legs in the water!
    By our boats we stay,
    Then swimming away
Come to us: it is forbidden!

        Come with us and play!
See, we are tall as women!

Our eyes are keen:
Our hair is bright:
Our voices speak outright:
We revel in the sea's green!
Come play:
It is forbidden!


## IMMORTAL

Yes, there is one thing braver than all flowers;
Richer than clear gems; wider than the sky;
Immortal and unchangeable; whose powers
Transcend reason, love and sanity!

And thou, beloved, art that godly thing!
Marvellous and terrible; in glance
An injured Juno roused against Heaven's King!
And thy name, lovely One, is Ignorance.


## MEZZO FORTE

Take that, damn you; and that!
And here's a rose
To make it right again!
God knows
I'm sorry, Grace; but then,
It's not my fault if you will be a cat.


## AN AFTER SONG

So art thou broken in upon me, Apollo,
Through a splendour of purple garments—
Held by the yellow-haired Clymène
To clothe the white of thy shoulders—
Bare from the day's leaping of horses.
This is strange to me, here in the modern twilight.

## CRUDE LAMENT

Mother of flames,
 The men that went ahunting
Are asleep in the snow drifts.
 You have kept the fire burning!
Crooked fingers that pull
Fuel from among the wet leaves,
 Mother of flames
 You have kept the fire burning!
The young wives have fallen asleep
With wet hair, weeping,
 Mother of flames!
The young men raised the heavy spears
And are gone prowling in the darkness.
 O mother of flames,
 You who have kept the fire burning!
 Lo, I am helpless!
Would God they had taken me with them!


## THE ORDEAL

O crimson salamander,
Because of love's whim
    sacred!
Swim
 the winding flame
 Predestined to disman him
And bring our fellow home to us again.

 Swim in with watery fang,
 Gnaw out and drown
The fire roots that circle him
Until the Hell-flower dies down
 And he comes home again.

 Aye, bring him home,
 O crimson salamander,
That I may see he is unchanged with burning—
Then have your will with him,
 O crimson salamander.

## PORTENT

Red cradle of the night,
    In you
    The dusky child
Sleeps fast till his might
    Shall be piled
Sinew on sinew.

Red cradle of the night,
    The dusky child
Sleeping sits upright.
    Lo how
        The winds blow now!
    He pillows back;
The winds are again mild.

When he stretches his arms out,
Red cradle of the night,
    The alarms shout
From bare tree to tree,
    Wild
        In afright!
Mighty shall he be,
Red cradle of the night,
    The dusky child ! !

## CON BRIO

Miserly, is the best description of that poor fool
Who holds Lancelot to have been a morose fellow,
Dolefully brooding over the events which had naturally to follow
The high time of his deed with Guinevere.
He has a sick historical sight, if I judge rightly,
To believe any such thing as that ever occurred.
But, by the god of blood, what else is it that has deterred
Us all from an out and out defiance of fear
But this same perdamnable miserliness,
Which cries about our necks how we shall have less and less
Than we have now if we spend too wantonly?

Bah, this sort of slither is below contempt!

In the same vein we should have apple trees exempt
From bearing anything but pink blossoms all the year,
Fixed permanent lest their bellies wax unseemly, and the dear
Innocent days of them be wasted quite.

How can we have less? Have we not the deed?

Lancelot thought little, spent his gold and rode to fight
Mounted, if God was willing, on a good steed.

## AD INFINITUM

Still I bring flowers
Although you fling them at my feet
Until none stays
That is not struck across with wounds:
Flowers and flowers
That you may break them utterly
As you have always done.

Sure happily
I still bring flowers, flowers,
Knowing how all
Are crumpled in your praise
And may not live
To speak a lesser thing.

## HIC JACET

The coroner's merry little children
Have such twinkling brown eyes.
Their father is not of gay men
And their mother jocular in no wise,
Yet the coroner's merry little children
Laugh so easily.

They laugh because they prosper.
Fruit for them is upon all branches.

Lo! how they jibe at loss, for
    Kind heaven fills their little paunches!
It's the coroner's merry, merry children
    Who laugh so easily.

## CONTEMPORANIA

The corner of a great rain
Steamy with the country
Has fallen upon my garden.

I go back and forth now
And the little leaves follow me
Talking of the great rain,
Of branches broken,
And the farmer's curses!

But I go back and forth
In this corner of a garden
And the green shoots follow me
Praising the great rain.

We are not curst together,
The leaves and I,
Framing devices, flower devices
And other ways of peopling
The barren country.

Truly it was a very great rain
That makes the little leaves follow me.

## TO WISH MYSELF COURAGE

On the day when youth is no more upon me
I will write of the leaves and the moon in a tree top!
I will sing then the song, long in the making—
When the stress of youth is put away from me.

How can I ever be written out as men say?
Surely it is merely an interference with the long song—
This that I am now doing.

But when the spring of it is worn like the old moon
And the eaten leaves are lace upon the cold earth—
Then I will rise up in my great desire—
Long at the birth—and sing me the youth-song!

# FROM "THE DIAL"

## PORTRAIT OF A LADY

Your thighs are appletrees
whose blossoms touch the sky.
Which sky? The sky
where Watteau hung a lady's
slipper. Your knees
are a southern breeze—or
a gust of snow. Agh! what
sort of man was Fragonard?
—As if that answered
anything.—Ah, yes. Below
the knees, since the tune
drops that way, it is
one of those white summer days,
the tall grass of your ankles
flickers upon the shore—
Which shore?—
the sand clings to my lips—
Which shore?
Agh, petals maybe. How
should I know?
Which shore? Which shore?
—the petals from some hidden
appletree—Which shore?
I said petals from an appletree.

## SPRING STORM

The sky has given over
its bitterness.
Out of the dark change
all day long
rain falls and falls
as if it would never end.
Still the snow keeps
its hold on the ground.
But water, water is seething
from a thousand runnels.
It collects swiftly,
dappled with black
cuts a way for itself
through green ice in the gutters.
Drop after drop it falls
from the withered grass stems
of the overhanging embankment.

# FROM "POETRY"

## LOVE SONG

What have I to say to you
When we shall meet?
Yet—
I lie here thinking of you.

The stain of love
Is upon the world.
Yellow, yellow, yellow,
It eats into the leaves,
Smears with saffron
The horned branches that lean
Heavily
Against a smooth purple sky.

There is no light—
Only a honey-thick stain
That drips from leaf to leaf
And limb to limb,
Spoiling the colors
Of the whole world.

I am alone.
The weight of love
Has buoyed me up
Till my head
Knocks against the sky.

See me!
My hair is dripping with nectar—

Starlings carry it
On their black wings.
See, at last
My arms and my hands
Are lying idle.

How can I tell
If I shall ever love you again
As I do now?


## NAKED

What fool would feel
His cheeks burn
Because of the snow?
Would he call it
By a name, give it
Breasts, features,
Bare limbs?
Would he call it
A woman?
(Surely then he would be
A fool.)

And see her,
Warmed with the cold,
Go upon the heads
Of creatures
Whose faces lean
To the ground?

Would he watch
The compassion of
Her eyes,
That look, now up
Now down,
To the turn of
The wind and
The turn of
The shivering minds

She touches—
Motionless—troubled?

    I ask you—
I ask you, my townspeople,
What fool is this?

    Would he forget
The sight of
His mother and
His wife
Because of her?—
Have his heart
Turned to ice
That will not soften?

    What!
Would he see a thing
Lovelier than
A high-school girl,
With the skill
Of Venus
To stand naked—
Naked on the air?

        Falling snow and
            *you up there—waiting.*


## MARRIAGE

    So different, this man
And this woman:
A stream flowing
In a field.


## APOLOGY

    Why do I write today?
The beauty of
The terrible faces

Of our nonentities
Stirs me to it:

Colored women
Day workers,
Old and experienced,
Returning home at dusk
In cast-off clothing,
Faces like
Old Florentine oak.

Also
The set pieces
Of your faces stir me —
Leading citizens:
But not
In the same way.

## SUMMER SONG

Wanderer moon,
Smiling
A faintly ironical smile
At this brilliant,
Dew-moistened
Summer morning —
A detached,
Sleepily indifferent
Smile,
A wanderer's smile —
If I should
Buy a shirt
Your color, and
Put on a necktie
Sky-blue,
Where would they carry me?
Over the hills and
Far away?
Where would they carry me?

## THE OLD WORSHIPPER

How times change, old friend,
And how little anything changes!

We used to collect butterflies
And insects in Kipp's woods—
Do you remember?
Now this wonderful collection
From the Amazon
Comes quite naturally
For you to weigh and to classify.

Quiet and unnoticed
The flower of your whole life
Has opened its perfect petals—
And none to witness, save one
Old worshipper!

# FROM "THE LITTLE REVIEW"

## TO MARK ANTHONY IN HEAVEN

This quiet morning light
reflected, how many times!
from grass and trees and clouds
enters my north room
touching the walls with
grass and clouds and trees,
Anthony,
trees and grass and clouds.
Why did you follow
that beloved body
with your ships at Actium?
I hope it was because
you knew her inch by inch
from slanting feet upward
to the roots of her hair
and down again and that
you saw her
above the battle's fury
reflecting—
clouds and trees and grass
for then
you are listening in heaven.

# FROM "SOUR GRAPES"

## THE WIDOW'S LAMENT IN SPRINGTIME

Sorrow is my own yard
where the new grass
flames as it has flamed
often before but not
with the cold fire
that closes round me this year.
Thirtyfive years
I lived with my husband.
The plumtree is white today
with masses of flowers.
Masses of flowers
load the cherry branches
and color some bushes
yellow and some red
but the grief in my heart
is stronger than they
for though they were my joy
formerly, today I notice them
and turn away forgetting.
Today my son told me
that in the meadows,
at the edge of the heavy woods
in the distance, he saw
trees of white flowers.
I feel that I would like
to go there
and fall into those flowers
and sink into the marsh near them.

## QUEEN-ANN'S-LACE

Her body is not so white as
anemony petals nor so smooth—nor
so remote a thing. It is a field
of the wild carrot taking
the field by force; the grass
does not raise above it.
Here is no question of whiteness,
white as can be, with a purple mole
at the center of each flower.
Each flower is a hand's span
of her whiteness. Wherever
his hand has lain there is
a tiny purple blemish. Each part
is a blossom under his touch
to which the fibres of her being
stem one by one, each to its end,
until the whole field is a
white desire, empty, a single stem,
a cluster, flower by flower,
a pious wish to whiteness gone over—
or nothing.

## THE LATE SINGER

Here it is spring again
and I still a young man!
I am late at my singing.
The sparrow with the black rain on his breast
has been at his cadenzas for two weeks past:
What is it that is dragging at my heart?
The grass by the back door
is stiff with sap.
The old maples are opening
their branches of brown and yellow moth-flowers.
A moon hangs in the blue
in the early afternoons over the marshes.
I am late at my singing.

## APRIL

If you had come away with me
into another state
we had been quiet together.
But there the sun coming up
out of the nothing beyond the lake was
too low in the sky,
there was too great a pushing
against him,
too much of sumac buds, pink
in the head
with the clear gum upon them,
too many opening hearts of
lilac leaves,
too many, too many swollen
limp poplar tassels on the
bare branches!
It was too strong in the air.
I had no rest against that
springtime!
The pounding of the hoofs on the
raw sods
stayed with me half through the night.
I awoke smiling but tired.

## A GOODNIGHT

Go to sleep—though of course you will not—
to tideless waves thundering slantwise against
strong embankments, rattle and swish of spray
dashed thirty feet high, caught by the lake wind,
scattered and strewn broadcast in over the steady
car rails! Sleep, sleep! Gulls' cries in a wind-gust
broken by the wind; calculating wings set above
the field of waves breaking.
Go to sleep to the lunge between foam-crests,
refuse churned in the recoil. Food! Food!
Offal! Offal! that holds them in the air, wave-white
for the one purpose, feather upon feather, the wild
chill in their eyes, the hoarseness in their voices—
sleep, sleep . . .

Gentlefooted crowds are treading out your lullaby.
Their arms nudge, they brush shoulders,
hitch this way then that, mass and surge at the crossings—
lullaby, lullaby! The wild-fowl police whistles,
the enraged roar of the traffic, machine shrieks:
it is all to put you to sleep,
to soften your limbs in relaxed postures,
and that your head slip sidewise, and your hair loosen
and fall over your eyes and over your mouth,
brushing your lips wistfully that you may dream,
sleep and dream—

A black fungus springs out about lonely church doors—
sleep, sleep. The Night, coming down upon
the wet boulevard, would start you awake with his
message, to have in at your window. Pay no
heed to him. He storms at your sill with
cooings, with gesticulations, curses!
You will not let him in. He would keep you from sleeping.
He would have you sit under your desk lamp
brooding, pondering; he would have you
slide out the drawer, take up the ornamented dagger
and handle it. It is late, it is nineteen-nineteen—
go to sleep, his cries are a lullaby;
his jabbering is a sleep-well-my-baby; he is
a crackbrained messenger.

The maid waking you in the morning
when you are up and dressing,
the rustle of your clothes as you raise them—
it is the same tune.
At table the cold, greenish, split grapefruit, its juice
on the tongue, the clink of the spoon in
your coffee, the toast odors say it over and over.

The open street-door lets in the breath of
the morning wind from over the lake.
The bus coming to a halt grinds from its sullen brakes—
lullaby, lullaby. The crackle of a newspaper,
the movement of the troubled coat beside you—
sleep, sleep, sleep, sleep . . .

It is the sting of snow, the burning liquor of
the moonlight, the rush of rain in the gutters packed
with dead leaves: go to sleep, go to sleep.
And the night passes—and never passes—

## OVERTURE TO A DANCE OF LOCOMOTIVES

### I

Men with picked voices chant the names
of cities in a huge gallery: promises
that pull through descending stairways
to a deep rumbling.
         The rubbing feet
of those coming to be carried quicken a
grey pavement into soft light that rocks
to and fro, under the domed ceiling,
across and across from pale
earthcoloured walls of bare limestone.

Covertly the hands of a great clock
go round and round! Were they to
move quickly and at once the whole
secret would be out and the shuffling
of all ants be done forever.

A leaning pyramid of sunlight, narrowing
out at a high window, moves by the clock:
disaccordant hands straining out from
a center: inevitable postures infinitely
repeated—

### II

Two—twofour—twoeight!
Porters in red hats run on narrow platforms.
This way ma'm!
         —important not to take
the wrong train!
         Lights from the concrete
ceiling hang crooked but—
         Poised horizontal

on glittering parallels the dingy cylinders
packed with a warm glow—inviting entry—
pull against the hour. But brakes can
hold a fixed posture till—
                              The whistle!

Not twoeight. Not twofour. Two!

Gliding windows. Colored cooks sweating
in a small kitchen. Taillights—

In time: twofour!
In time: twoeight!

—rivers are tunneled: trestles
cross oozy swampland: wheels repeating
the same gesture remain relatively
stationary: rails forever parallel
return on themselves infinitely.
                              The dance is sure.


## THE DESOLATE FIELD

        Vast and grey, the sky
        is a simulacrum
        to all but him whose days
        are vast and grey, and—
        In the tall, dried grasses
        a goat stirs
        with nozzle searching the ground.
        —my head is in the air
        but who am I . . ?
        And amazed my heart leaps
        at the thought of love
        vast and grey
        yearning silently over me.

## WILLOW POEM

It is a willow when summer is over,
a willow by the river
from which no leaf has fallen nor
bitten by the sun
turned orange or crimson.
The leaves cling and grow paler,
swing and grow paler
over the swirling waters of the river
as if loath to let go,
they are so cool, so drunk with
the swirl of the wind and of the river—
oblivious to winter,
the last to let go and fall
into the water and on the ground.

## JANUARY

Again I reply to the triple winds
running chromatic fifths of derision
outside my window:
                    Play louder.
You will not succeed. I am
bound more to my sentences
the more you batter at me
to follow you.
              And the wind,
as before, fingers perfectly
its derisive music.

## BLIZZARD

Snow:
years of anger following
hours that float idly down—
the blizzard
drifts its weight
deeper and deeper for three days
or sixty years, eh? Then
  the sun! a clutter of

yellow and blue flakes—
Hairy looking trees stand out
in long alleys
over a wild solitude.
The man turns and there—
his solitary track stretched out
upon the world.

## TO WAKEN AN OLD LADY

Old age is
a flight of small
cheeping birds
skimming
bare trees
above a snow glaze.
Gaining and failing
they are buffetted
by a dark wind—
But what?
On harsh weedstalks
the flock has rested,
the snow
is covered with broken
seedhusks
and the wind tempered
by a shrill
piping of plenty.

## WINTER TREES

All the complicated details
of the attiring and
the disattiring are completed!
A liquid moon
moves gently among
the long branches.
Thus having prepared their buds
against a sure winter
the wise trees
stand sleeping in the cold.

## COMPLAINT

They call me and I go
It is a frozen road
past midnight, a dust
of snow caught
in the rigid wheeltracks.
The door opens.
I smile, enter and
shake off the cold.
Here is a great woman
on her side in the bed.
She is sick,
perhaps vomiting,
perhaps laboring
to give birth to
a tenth child. Joy! Joy!
Night is a room
darkened for lovers,
through the jalousies the sun
has sent one gold needle!
I pick the hair from her eyes
and watch her misery
with compassion.

## THE COLD NIGHT

It is cold. The white moon
is up among her scattered stars—
like the bare thighs of
the Police Sergeant's wife—among
her five children . . .
No answer. Pale shadows lie upon
the frosted grass. One answer:
It is midnight, it is still
and it is cold . . . !
White thighs of the sky! a
new answer out of the depths of
my male belly: In April . . .
In April I shall see again—In April!

the round and perfect thighs
of the Police Sergeant's wife
perfect still after many babies.
Oya!

### THURSDAY

I have had my dream—like others—
and it has come to nothing, so that
I remain now carelessly
with feet planted on the ground
and look up at the sky—
feeling my clothes about me,
the weight of my body in my shoes,
the rim of my hat, air passing in and out
at my nose—and decide to dream no more.

### THE POOR

By constantly tormenting them
with reminders of the lice in
their children's hair, the
School Physician first
brought their hatred down on him,
But by this familiarity
they grew used to him, and so,
at last,
took him for their friend and adviser.

### COMPLETE DESTRUCTION

It was an icy day.
We buried the cat,
then took her box
and set fire to it
in the back yard.
Those fleas that escaped
earth and fire
died by the cold.

## DAISY

The dayseye hugging the earth
in August, ha! Spring is
gone down in purple,
weeds stand high in the corn,
the rainbeaten furrow
is clotted with sorrel
and crabgrass, the
branch is black under
the heavy mass of the leaves—
The sun is upon a
slender green stem
ribbed lengthwise.
He lies on his back—
it is a woman also—
he regards his former
majesty and
round the yellow center,
split and creviced and done into
minute flowerheads, he sends out
his twenty rays—a little
and the wind is among them
to grow cool there!

One turns the thing over
in his hand and looks
at it from the rear: brownedged,
green and pointed scales
armor his yellow.
But turn and turn,
the crisp petals remain
brief, translucent, greenfastened,
barely touching at the edges:
blades of limpid seashell.

## THE THINKER

My wife's new pink slippers
have gay pom-poms.
There is not a spot or a stain
on their satin toes or their sides.
All night they lie together
under her bed's edge.
Shivering I catch sight of them
and smile, in the morning.
Later I watch them
descending the stair,
hurrying through the doors
and round the table,
moving stiffly
with a shake of their gay pom-poms!
And I talk to them
in my secret mind
out of pure happiness.

## THE LONELY STREET

School is over. It is too hot
to walk at ease. At ease
in light frocks they walk the streets
to while the time away.
They have grown tall. They hold
pink flames in their right hands.
In white from head to foot,
with sidelong, idle look—
in yellow, floating stuff,
black sash and stockings—
touching their avid mouths
with pink sugar on a stick—
like a carnation each holds in her hand—
they mount the lonely street.

## THE GREAT FIGURE

Among the rain
and lights
I saw the figure 5
in gold
on a red
firetruck
moving
with weight and urgency
tense
unheeded
to gong clangs
siren howls
and wheels rumbling
through the dark city.

## PORTRAIT OF THE AUTHOR

The birches are mad with green points
the wood's edge is burning with their green,
burning, seething—No, no, no.
The birches are opening their leaves one
by one. Their delicate leaves unfold cold
and separate, one by one. Slender tassels
hang swaying from the delicate branch tips—
Oh, I cannot say it. There is no word.
Black is split at once into flowers. In
every bog and ditch, flares of
small fire, white flowers!—Agh,
the birches are mad, mad with their green.
The world is gone, torn into shreds
with this blessing. What have I left undone
that I should have undertaken?

O my brother, you redfaced, living man
ignorant, stupid whose feet are upon
this same dirt that I touch—and eat.
We are alone in this terror, alone,
face to face on this road, you and I,
wrapped by this flame!

Let the polished plows stay idle,
their gloss already on the black soil.
But that face of yours—!
Answer me. I will clutch you. I
will hug you, grip you. I will poke my face
into your face and force you to see me.
Take me in your arms, tell me the commonest
thing that is in your mind to say,
say anything. I will understand you—!
It is the madness of the birch leaves opening
cold, one by one.

My rooms will receive me. But my rooms
are no longer sweet spaces where comfort
is ready to wait on me with its crumbs.
A darkness has brushed them. The mass
of yellow tulips in the bowl is shrunken.
Every familiar object is changed and dwarfed.
I am shaken, broken against a might
that splits comfort, blows apart
my careful partitions, crushes my house
and leaves me—with shrinking heart
and startled, empty eyes—peering out
into a cold world.

In the spring I would drink! In the spring
I would be drunk and lie forgetting all things.
Your face! Give me your face, Yang Kue Fei!
your hands, your lips to drink!
Give me your wrists to drink—
I drag you, I am drowned in you, you
overwhelm me! Drink!
Save me! The shad bush is in the edge
of the clearing. The yards in a fury
of lilac blossoms are driving me mad with terror.
Drink and lie forgetting the world.

And coldly the birch leaves are opening one by one.
Coldly I observe them and wait for the end.
And it ends.